Guest Name & Address

Thoughts & Best Wishes

AF094588

Guest Name & Address

Thoughts & Best Wishes

Guest Name & Address

Thoughts & Best Wishes

Guest Name & Address	Thoughts & Best Wishes

Guest Name & Address   Thoughts & Best Wishes

Guest Name & Address | Thoughts & Best Wishes

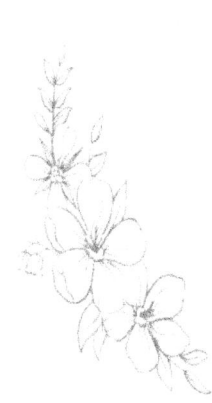 

Guest Name & Address

Thoughts & Best Wishes

Guest Name & Address

Thoughts & Best Wishes

Guest Name & Address

Thoughts & Best Wishes

Guest Name & Address

Thoughts & Best Wishes

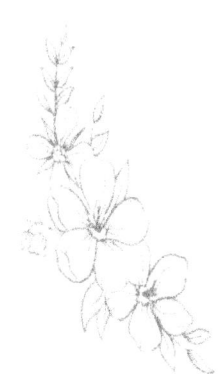

Guest Name & Address

Thoughts & Best Wishes

Guest Name & Address

Thoughts & Best Wishes

Guest Name & Address	Thoughts & Best Wishes

Guest Name & Address	Thoughts & Best Wishes

Guest Name & Address

Thoughts & Best Wishes

Guest Name & Address	Thoughts & Best Wishes

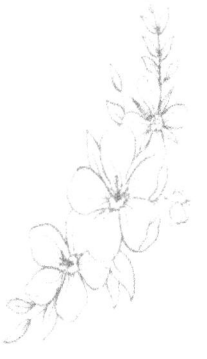

Guest Name & Address

Thoughts & Best Wishes

Guest Name & Address

Thoughts & Best Wishes

Guest Name & Address | Thoughts & Best Wishes

Guest Name & Address

Thoughts & Best Wishes

Guest Name & Address

Thoughts & Best Wishes

Guest Name & Address   Thoughts & Best Wishes

Guest Name & Address

Thoughts & Best Wishes

Guest Name & Address

Thoughts & Best Wishes

Guest Name & Address *Thoughts & Best Wishes*

Guest Name & Address   Thoughts & Best Wishes

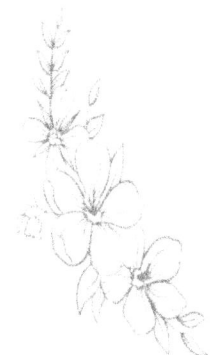

Guest Name & Address

Thoughts & Best Wishes

Guest Name & Address

Thoughts & Best Wishes

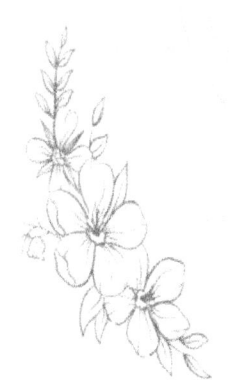

Guest Name & Address

Thoughts & Best Wishes

Guest Name & Address	Thoughts & Best Wishes

Guest Name & Address	Thoughts & Best Wishes

Guest Name & Address

Thoughts & Best Wishes

Guest Name & Address   Thoughts & Best Wishes

Guest Name & Address	Thoughts & Best Wishes

Guest Name & Address

Thoughts & Best Wishes

Guest Name & Address

Thoughts & Best Wishes

Guest Name & Address   Thoughts & Best Wishes

Guest Name & Address | Thoughts & Best Wishes

Guest Name & Address

Thoughts & Best Wishes

| Guest Name & Address | Thoughts & Best Wishes |
|---|---|ими
| | |

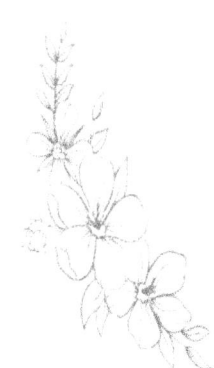

Guest Name & Address

Thoughts & Best Wishes

Guest Name & Address

Thoughts & Best Wishes

Guest Name & Address	Thoughts & Best Wishes

Guest Name & Address

Thoughts & Best Wishes

Guest Name & Address	Thoughts & Best Wishes

Guest Name & Address | Thoughts & Best Wishes

Guest Name & Address	Thoughts & Best Wishes

Guest Name & Address

Thoughts & Best Wishes

Guest Name & Address	Thoughts & Best Wishes

Guest Name & Address	Thoughts & Best Wishes

Guest Name & Address   Thoughts & Best Wishes

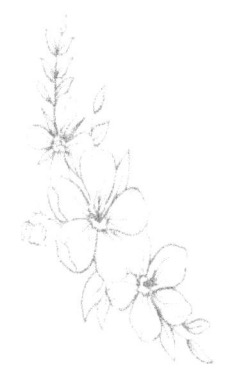

Guest Name & Address

Thoughts & Best Wishes

Guest Name & Address	Thoughts & Best Wishes

Guest Name & Address

Thoughts & Best Wishes

Guest Name & Address   Thoughts & Best Wishes

Guest Name & Address

Thoughts & Best Wishes

Guest Name & Address

Thoughts & Best Wishes

Guest Name & Address	Thoughts & Best Wishes

Guest Name & Address

Thoughts & Best Wishes

Guest Name & Address	Thoughts & Best Wishes

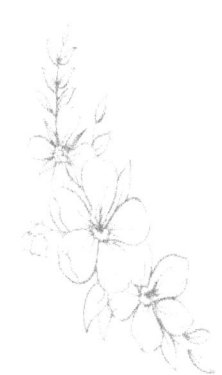

Guest Name & Address

Thoughts & Best Wishes

Guest Name & Address	Thoughts & Best Wishes

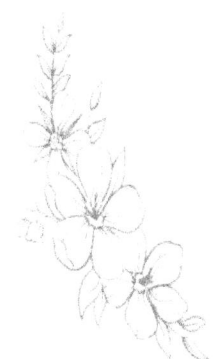

Guest Name & Address

Thoughts & Best Wishes

Guest Name & Address	Thoughts & Best Wishes

Guest Name & Address | *Thoughts & Best Wishes*

Guest Name & Address

Thoughts & Best Wishes

Guest Name & Address

Thoughts & Best Wishes

Guest Name & Address

Thoughts & Best Wishes

Guest Name & Address

Thoughts & Best Wishes

Guest Name & Address   Thoughts & Best Wishes

Guest Name & Address

Thoughts & Best Wishes

Guest Name & Address

Thoughts & Best Wishes

Guest Name & Address   Thoughts & Best Wishes

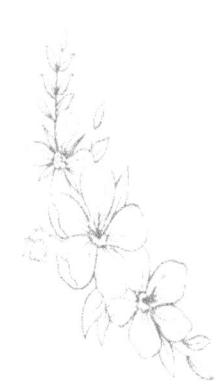

Guest Name & Address		Thoughts & Best Wishes

Guest Name & Address

Thoughts & Best Wishes

Guest Name & Address

Thoughts & Best Wishes

Guest Name & Address

Thoughts & Best Wishes

Guest Name & Address

Thoughts & Best Wishes

Guest Name & Address

Thoughts & Best Wishes

Guest Name & Address

Thoughts & Best Wishes

Guest Name & Address	Thoughts & Best Wishes

Guest Name & Address

Thoughts & Best Wishes

Guest Name & Address

Thoughts & Best Wishes

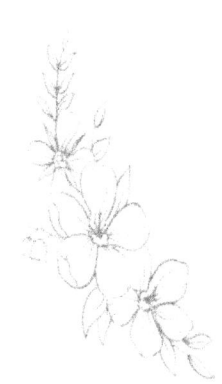

Guest Name & Address	Thoughts & Best Wishes

Guest Name & Address

Thoughts & Best Wishes

Guest Name & Address

Thoughts & Best Wishes

Guest Name & Address

Thoughts & Best Wishes

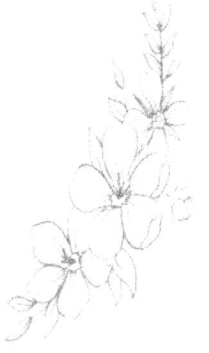

Guest Name & Address

Thoughts & Best Wishes

Guest Name & Address | Thoughts & Best Wishes

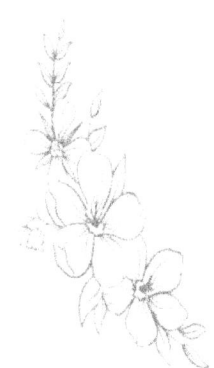

Guest Name & Address

Thoughts & Best Wishes

Guest Name & Address	Thoughts & Best Wishes

Guest Name & Address

Thoughts & Best Wishes

Guest Name & Address	Thoughts & Best Wishes

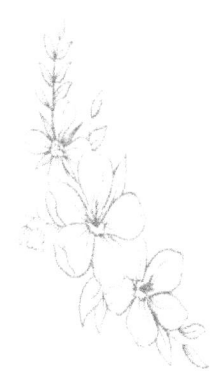

Guest Name & Address	Thoughts & Best Wishes

Guest Name & Address	Thoughts & Best Wishes

Guest Name & Address | *Thoughts & Best Wishes*

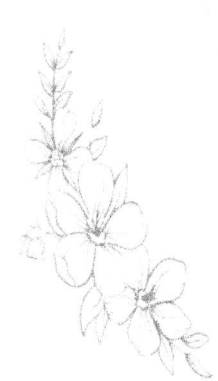 

Guest Name & Address	Thoughts & Best Wishes

Guest Name & Address	Thoughts & Best Wishes

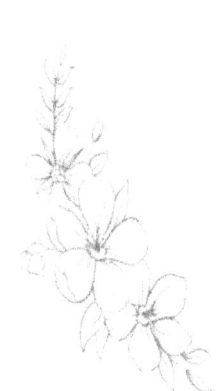

Guest Name & Address

Thoughts & Best Wishes

Guest Name & Address

Thoughts & Best Wishes

Guest Name & Address

Thoughts & Best Wishes

Guest Name & Address

Thoughts & Best Wishes

Guest Name & Address

Thoughts & Best Wishes

| Guest Name & Address | Thoughts & Best Wishes |
| --- | --- |//
| | |

Guest Name & Address

Thoughts & Best Wishes

Guest Name & Address	Thoughts & Best Wishes

Guest Name & Address	Thoughts & Best Wishes

www.ingramcontent.com/pod-product-compliance
Lightning Source LLC
LaVergne TN
LVHW060326080526
838202LV00053B/4426